Dear frien
parents and t

Welcome to the amazing world of transport, adventure and fun tasks!
This book is specifically designed for children who are just learning how to write.
You can travel through its pages, color in cars, solve interesting puzzles
and masterfully draw paths!

That's what makes it special.

Here are some **unique lines** for the track! They are not straight -
they go up and down, widen and narrow. The task is to draw a line neatly,
touching the borders of the track. This is not only exciting,
but it will also help to develop handwriting, improve
coordination of movements, and prepare the hand for writing.

And you are also waiting for:

Cool coloring pages with cars, planes, ships and other types of transport!

Intellectual challenges to sharpen your focus and cognitive abilities!

Exercises for **practicing working with scissors!**
Cut out the details and glue them in the right places.

Ready to go on a journey?
Then grab your pencils, markers, scissors and glue – and let's go on an adventure!

Good luck!

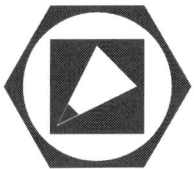

author and illustrator of the book

sweta
m o l o t o w a

Help the car get home.

Cut out
the parts of the road
and glue them
in the correct order.

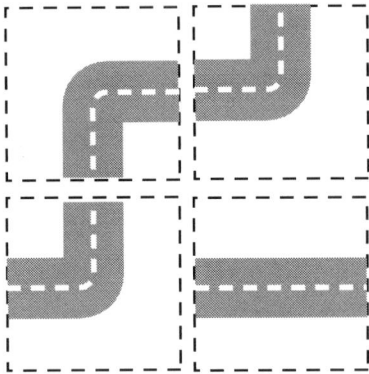

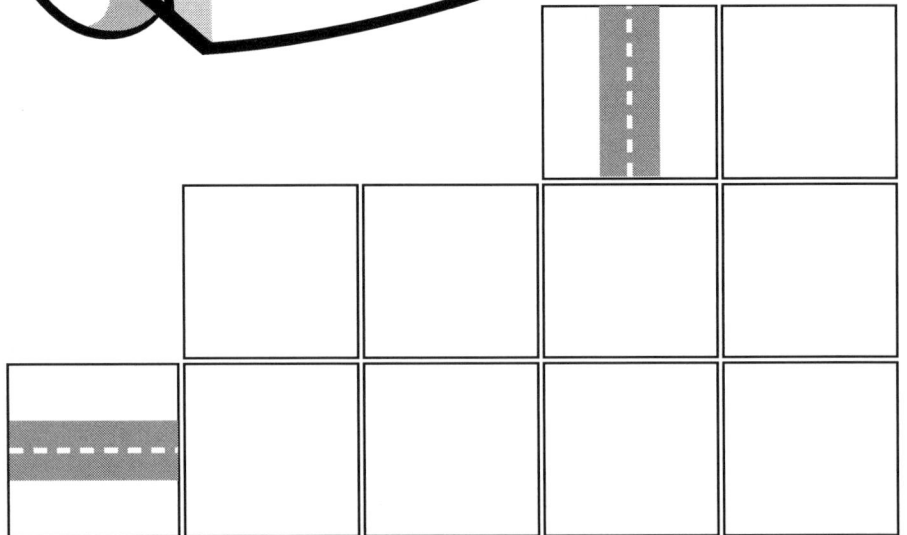

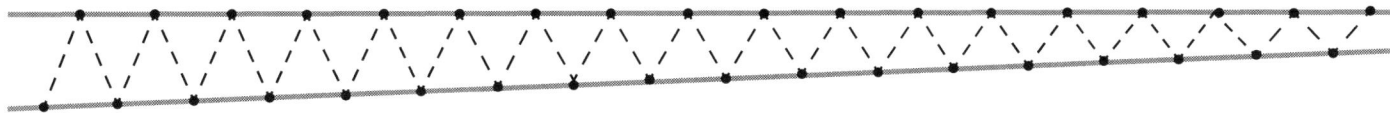
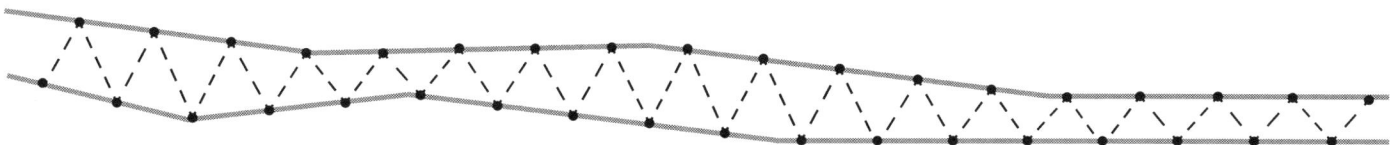
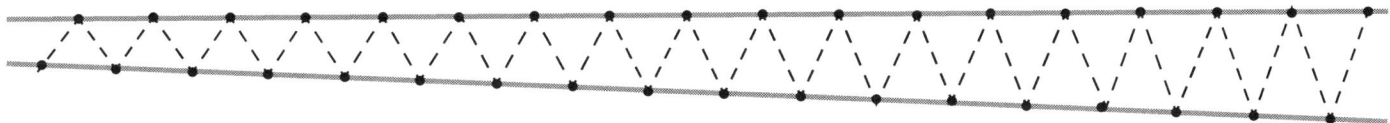

3

The plane is flying high in the sky.

Mark the clouds of the same shape
with their corresponding numbers.

1 2

3 4 5

4

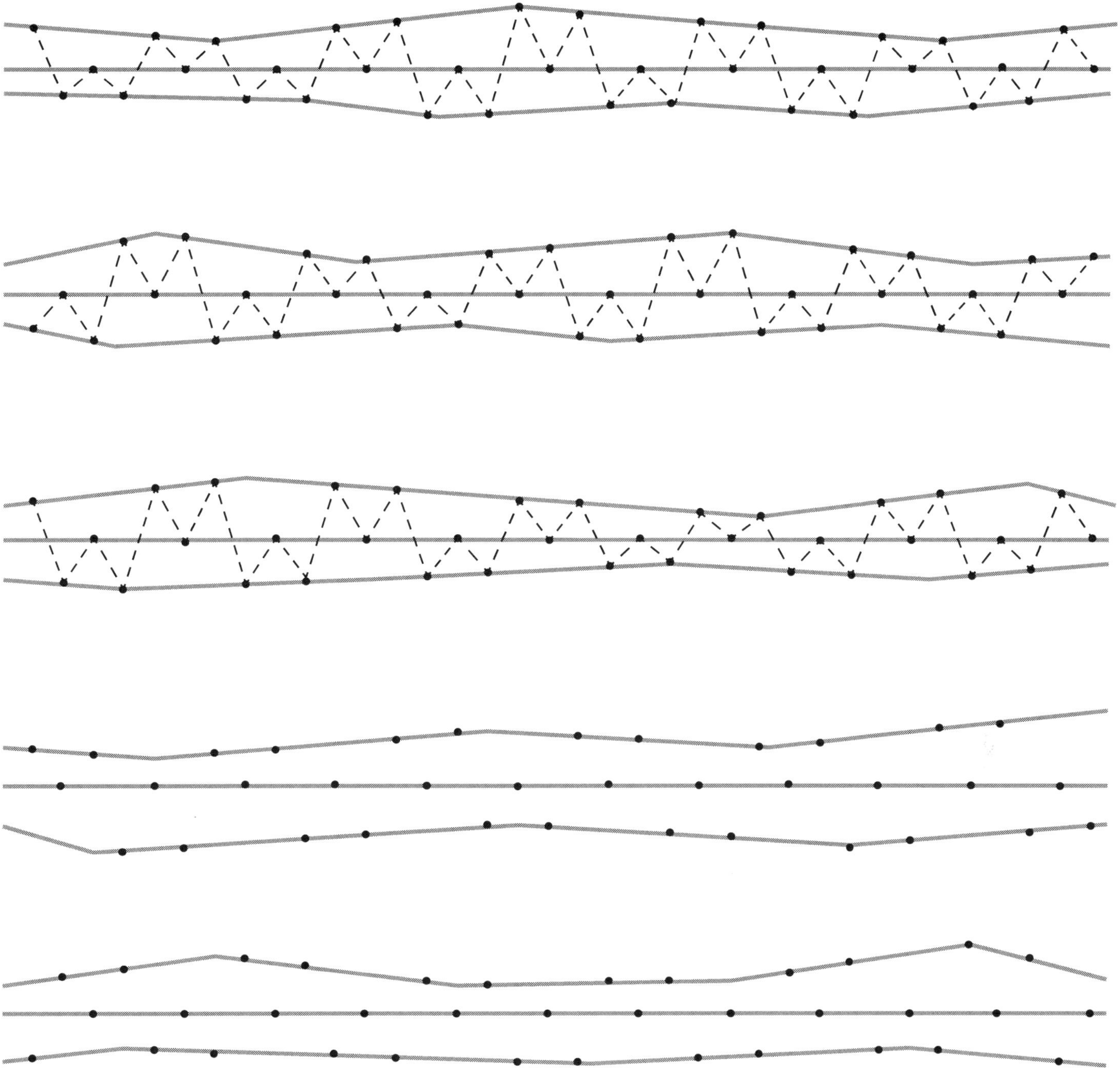

Repair the ship.

Cut out the squares below and stick them in the correct places.

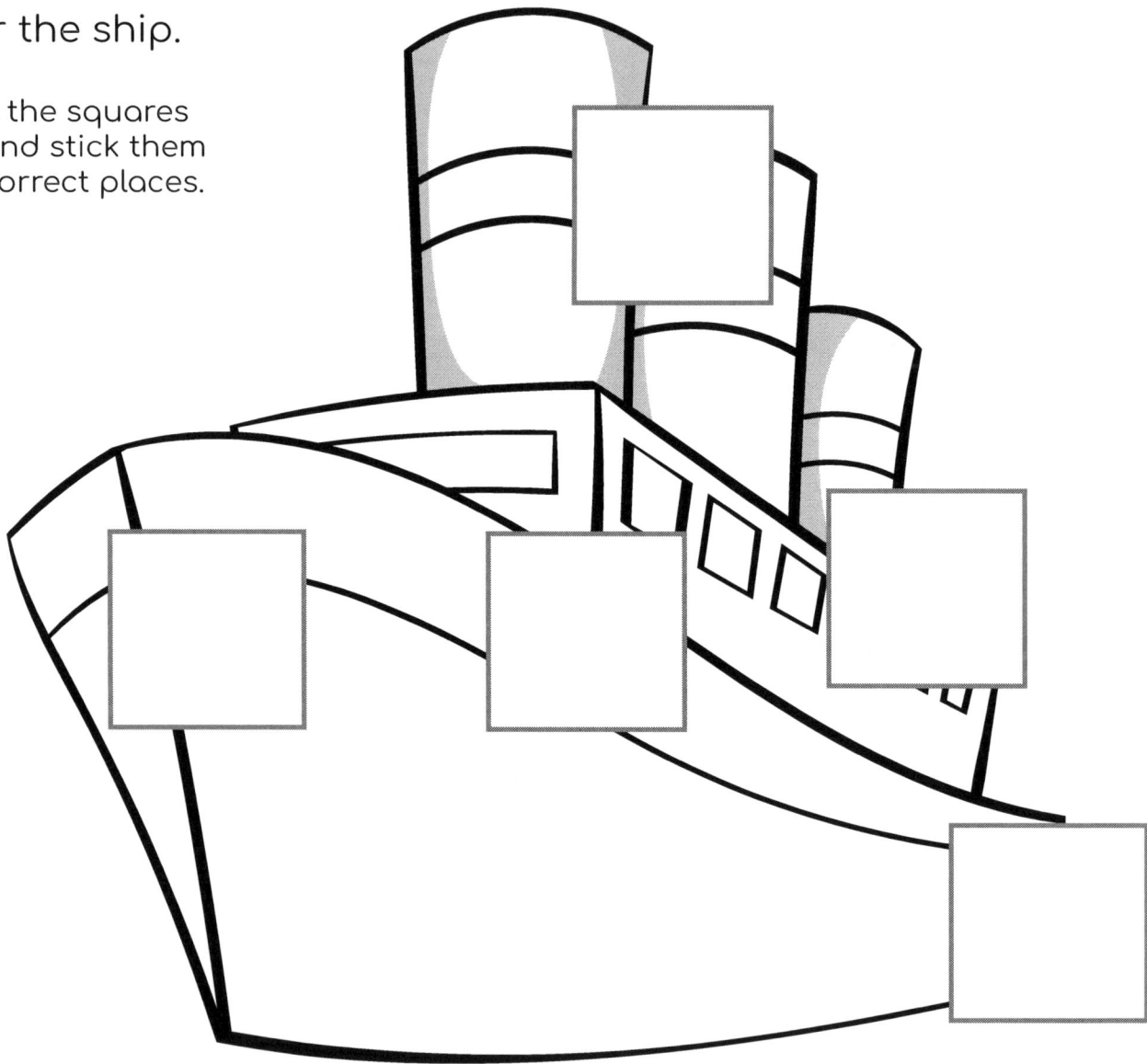

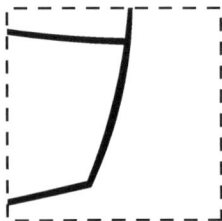

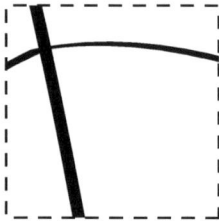

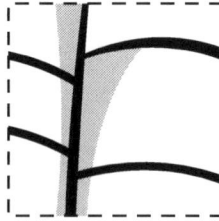

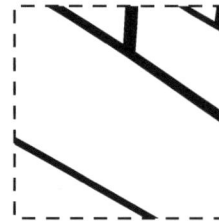

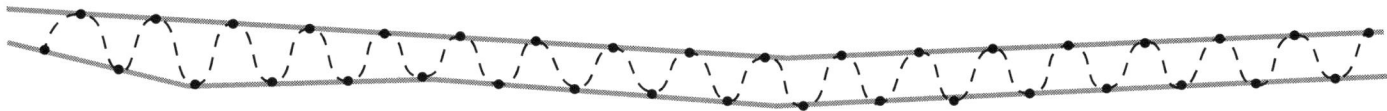

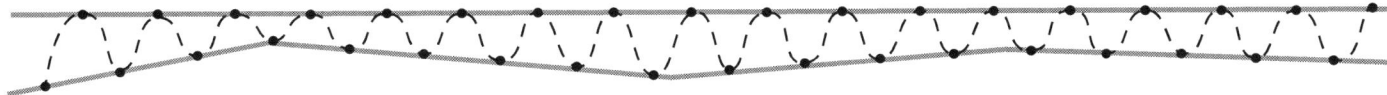

7

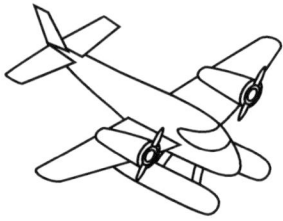

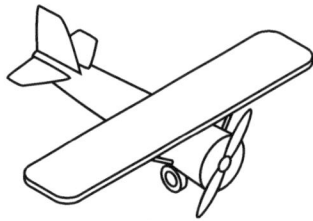

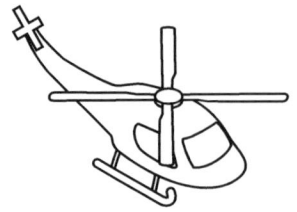

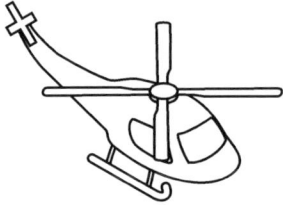

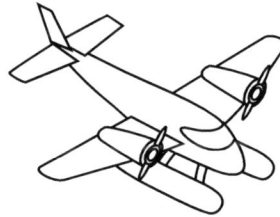

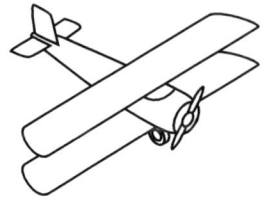

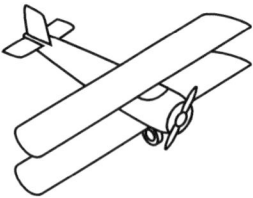

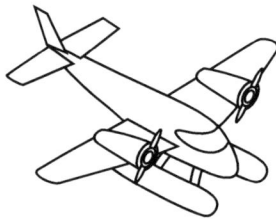

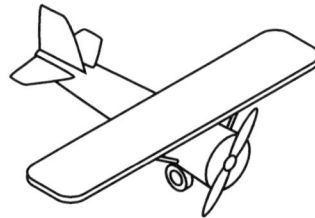

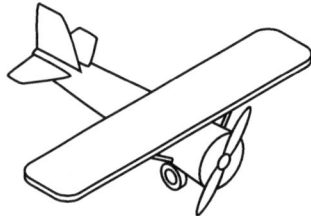

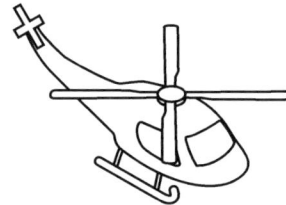

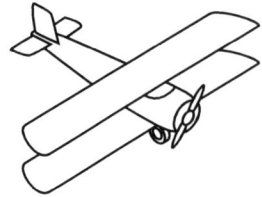

An airplane fell out of each row. Which one do you think?

Cut out the squares and glue the plane in place.

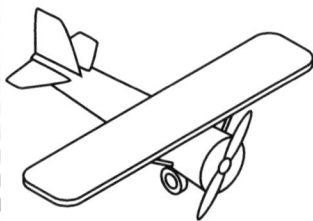

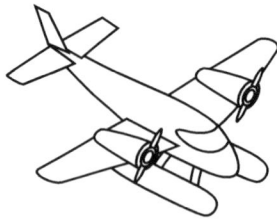

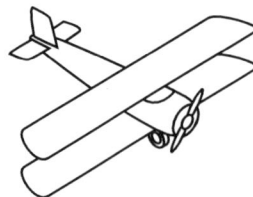

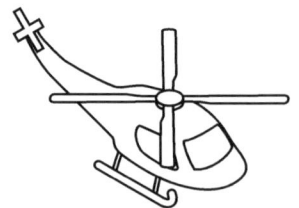

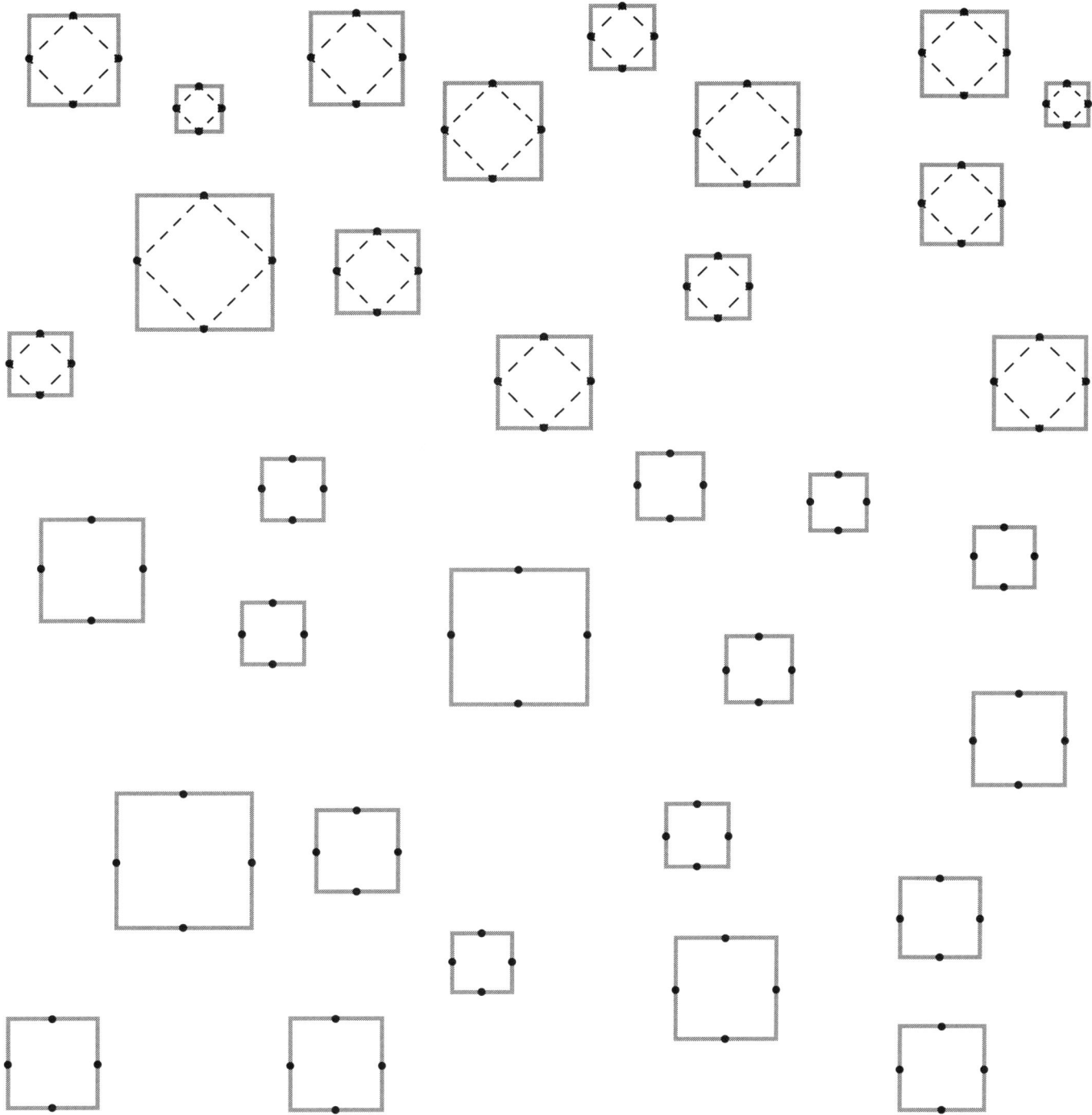

Shade the circles in the direction the arrow.

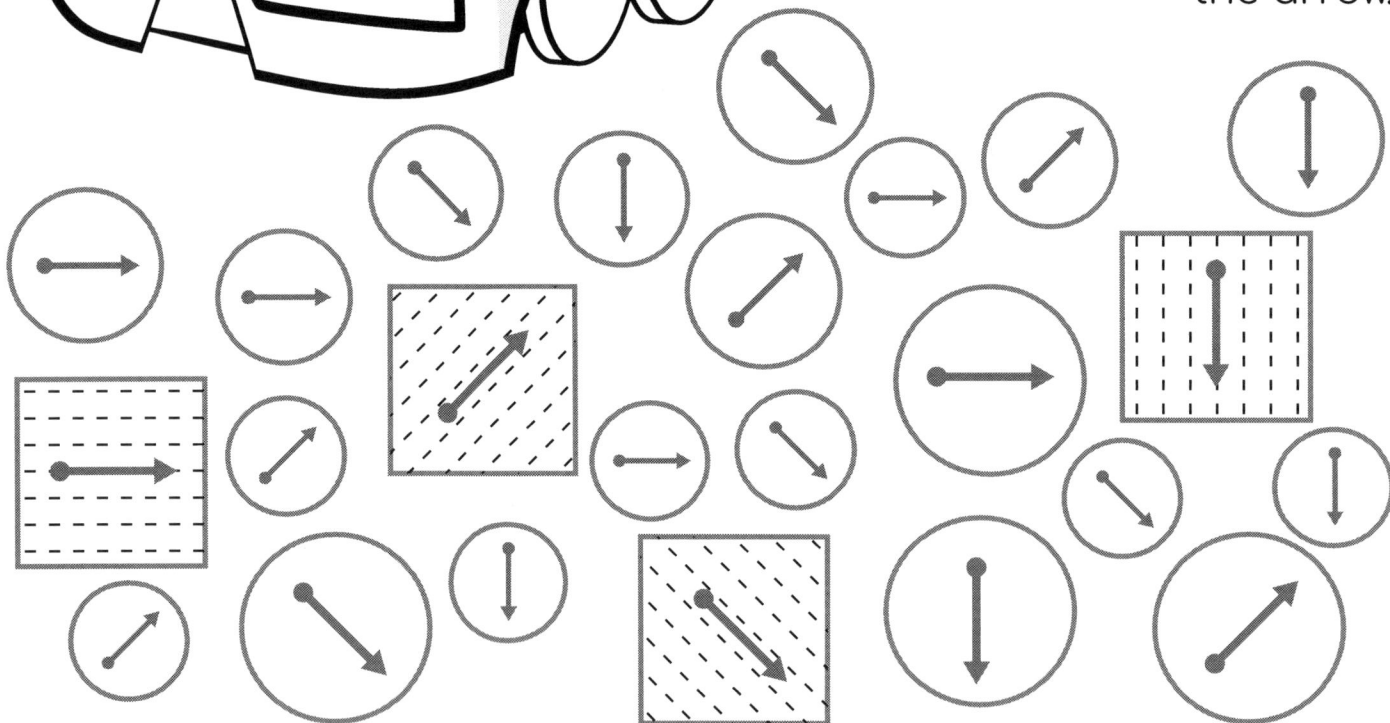

10

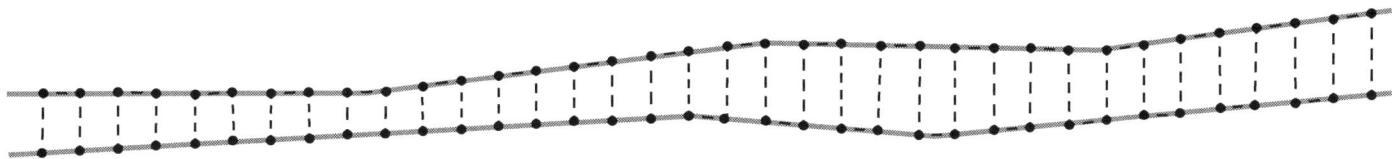

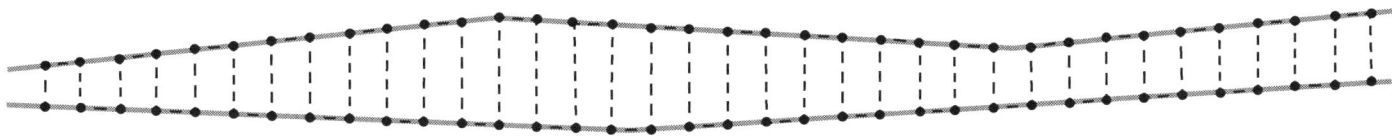

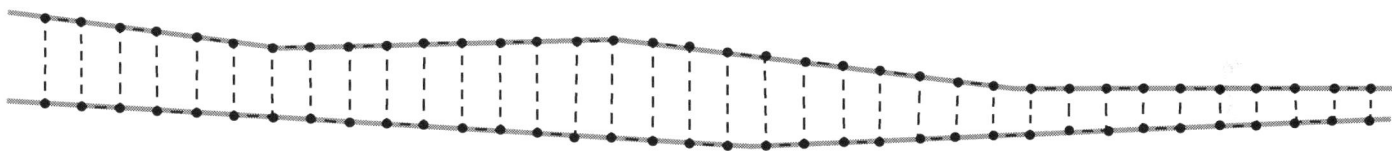

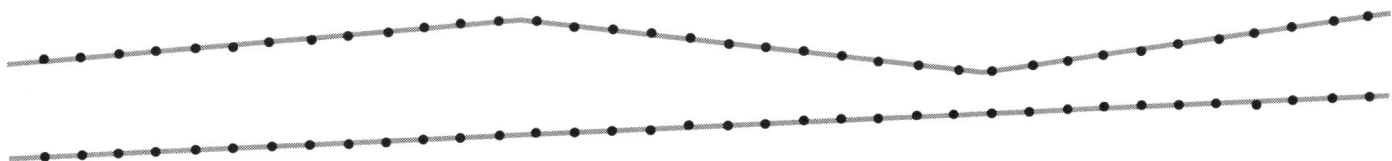

Repair the bus.

Cut out the squares and stick them in the correct places.

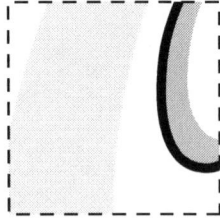

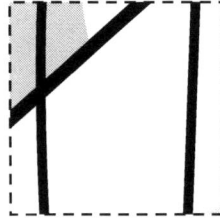

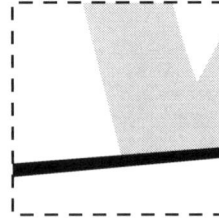

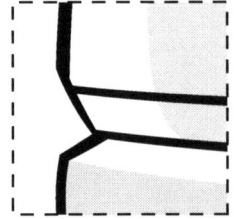

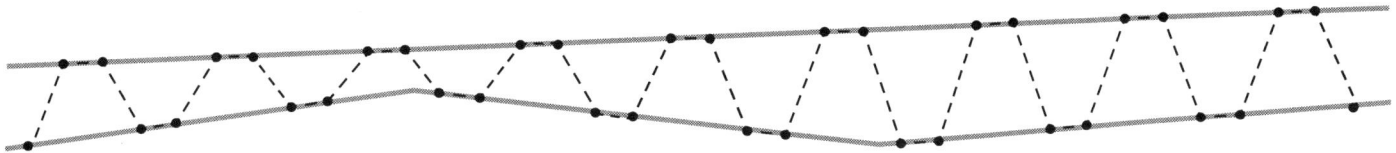

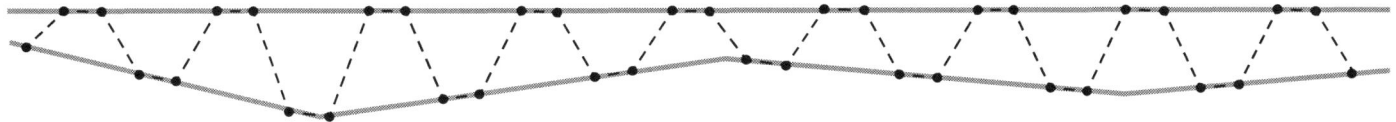

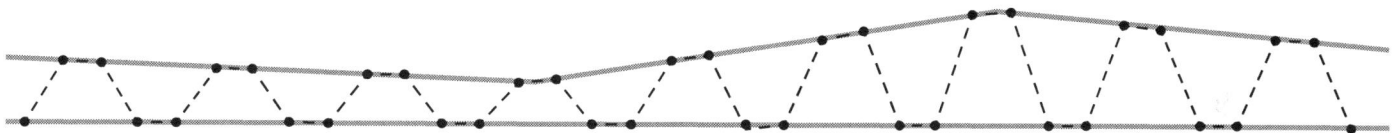

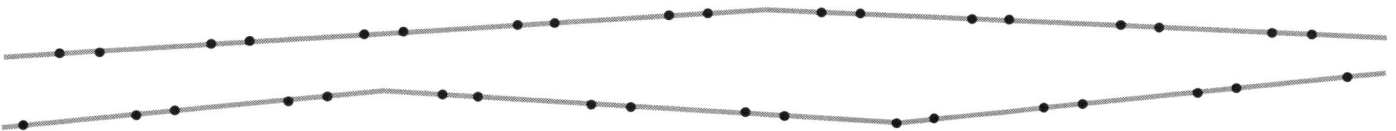

13

The rocket flew into space.

Count how many stars and planets it meets on its way.

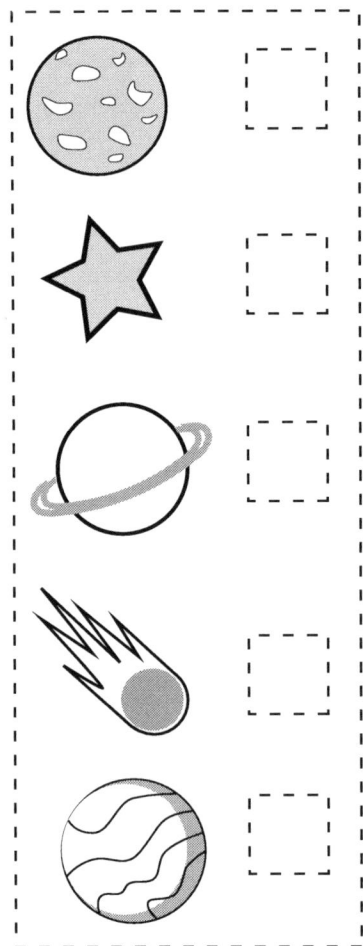

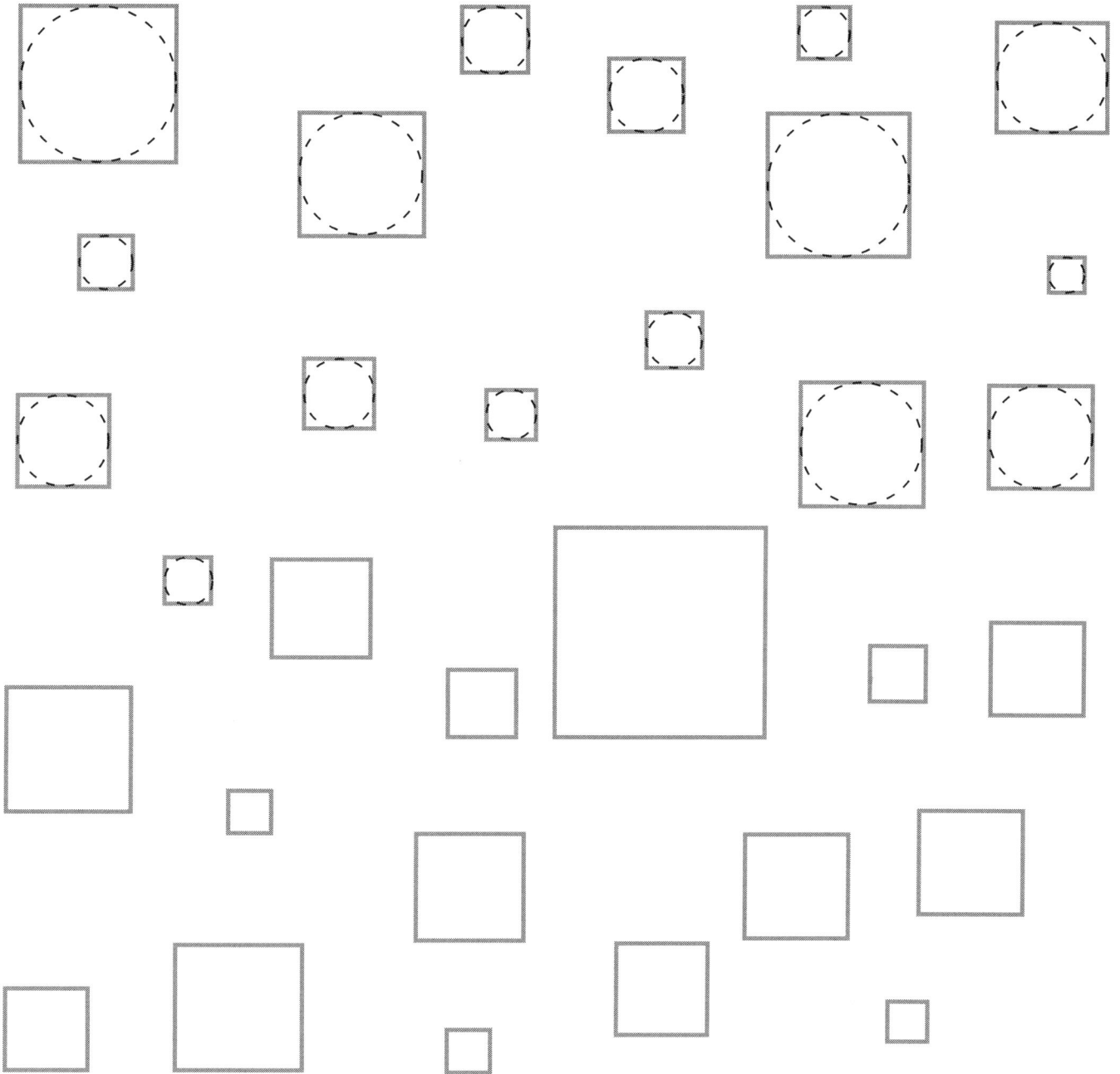

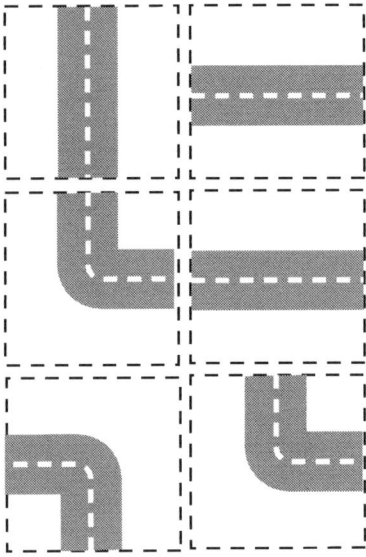

Help the bike get home.

Cut out the parts of the road
and glue them in the correct order.

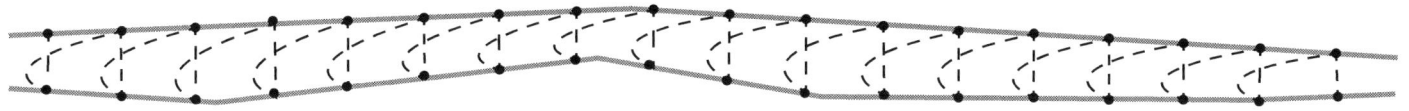

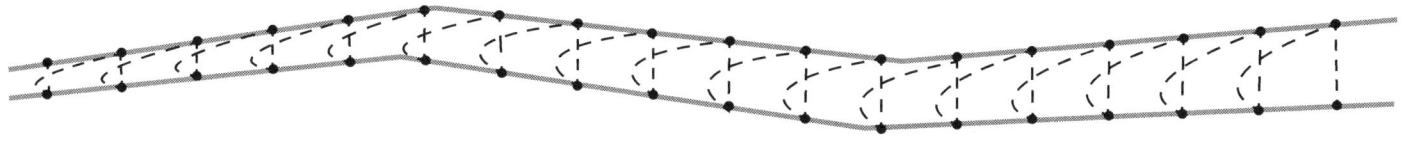

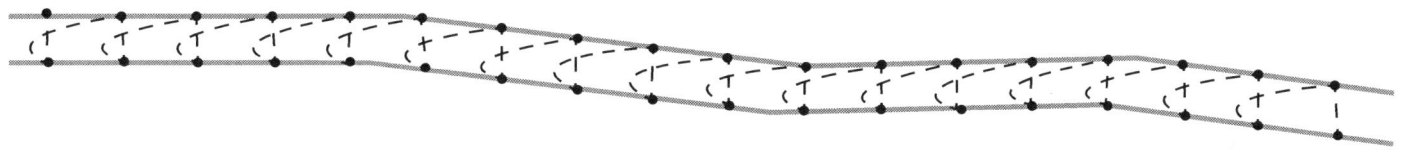

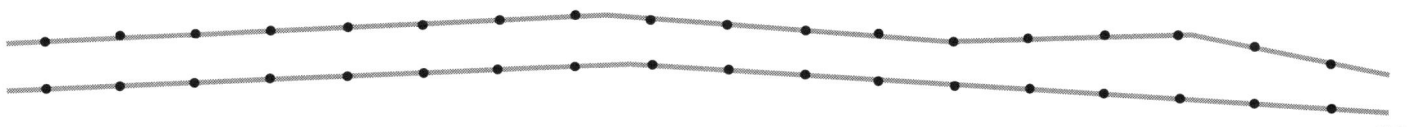

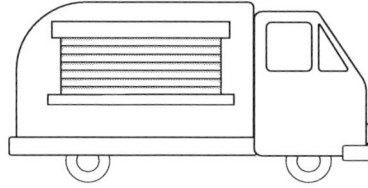

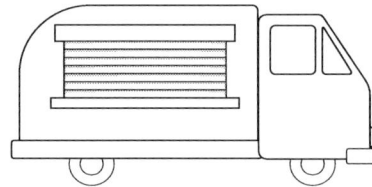

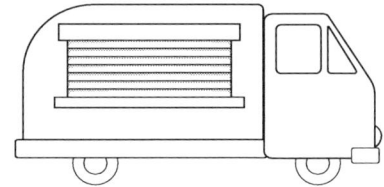

A car fell out of each row. Which one do you think?

Cut out the squares and glue the auto in place.

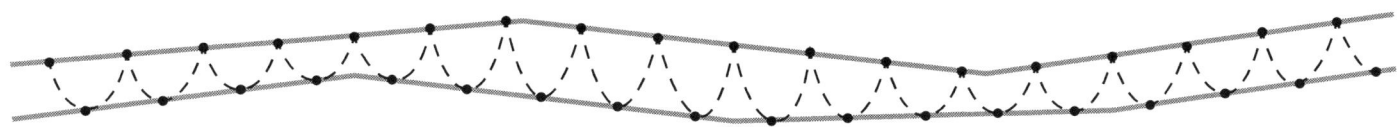

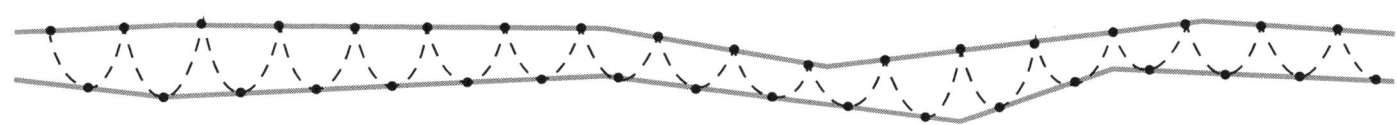

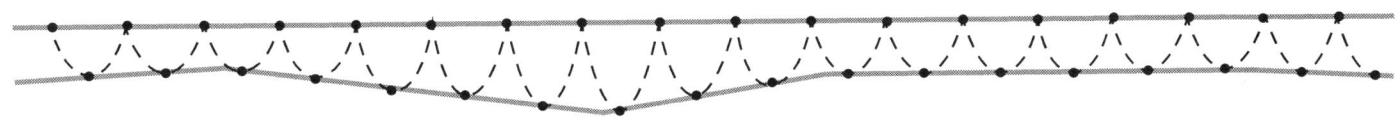

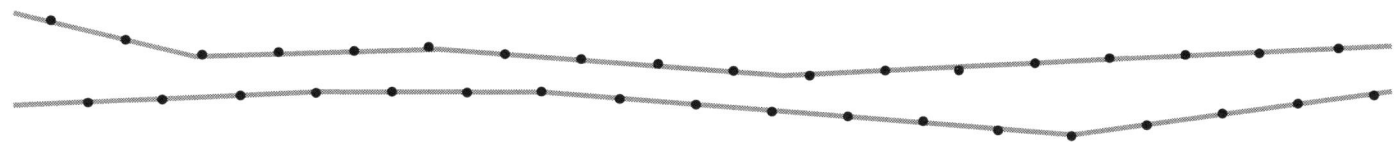

19

Match the birds
on the left with
the same order
on the right.

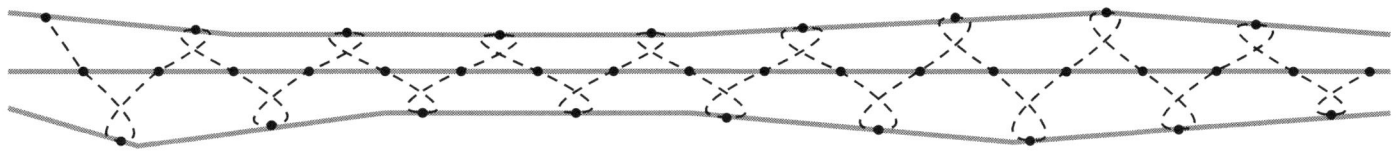

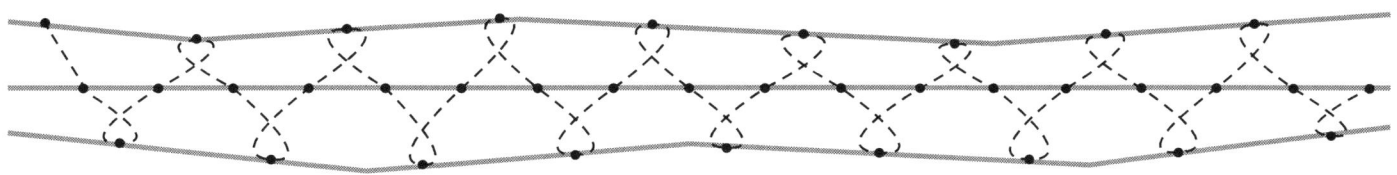

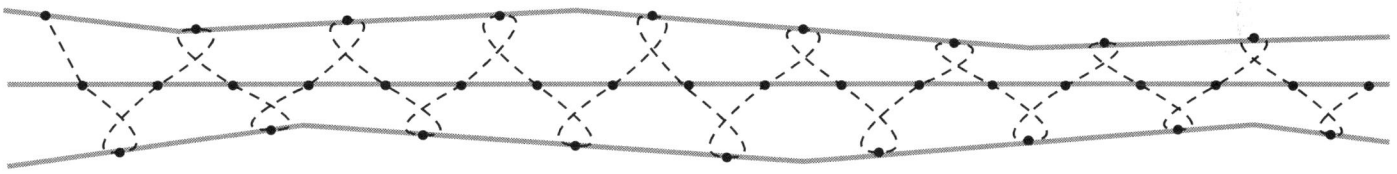

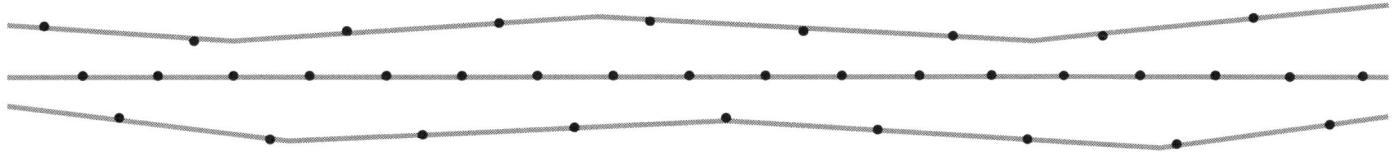

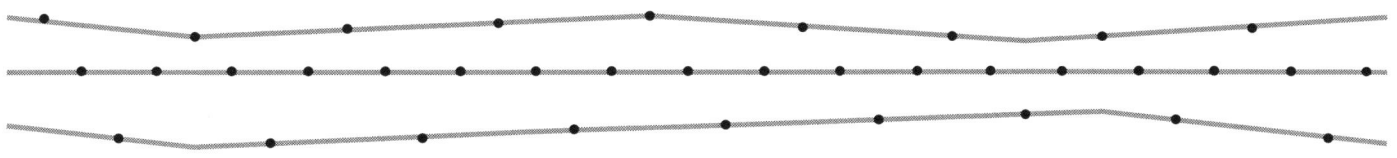

21

Repair the truck.

Cut out the squares and stick them in the correct places.

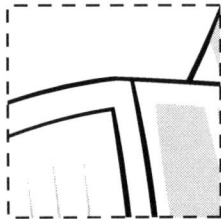

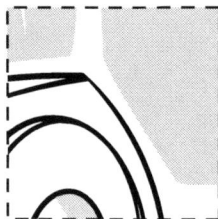

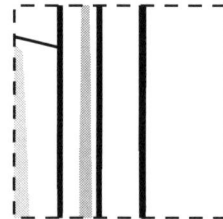

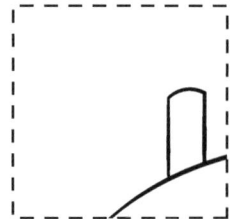

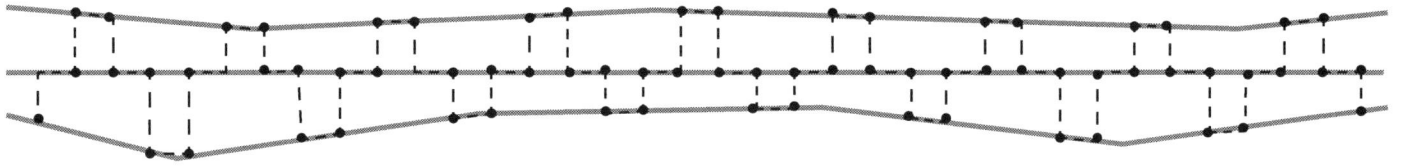

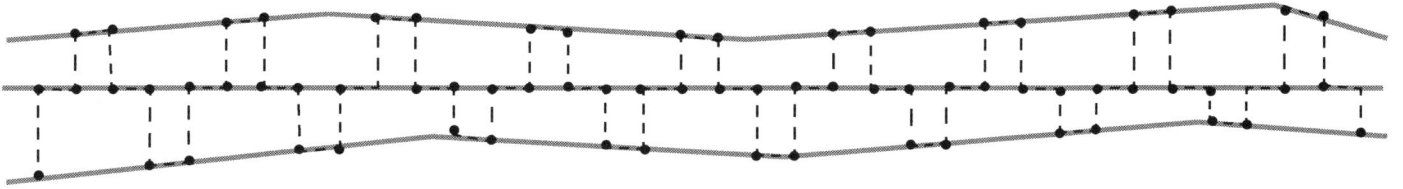

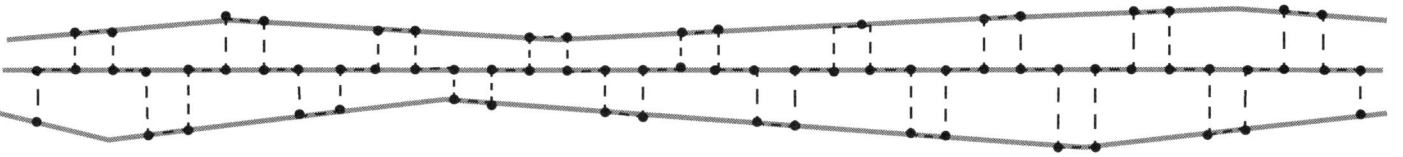

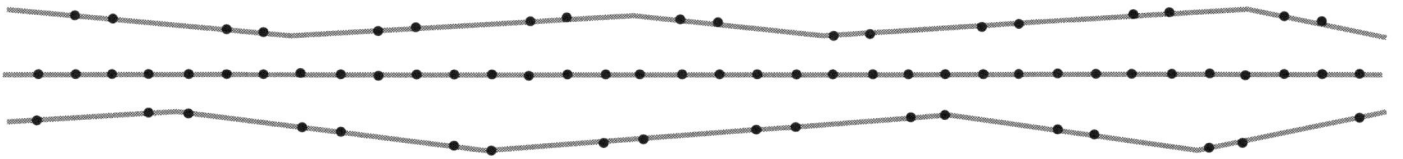

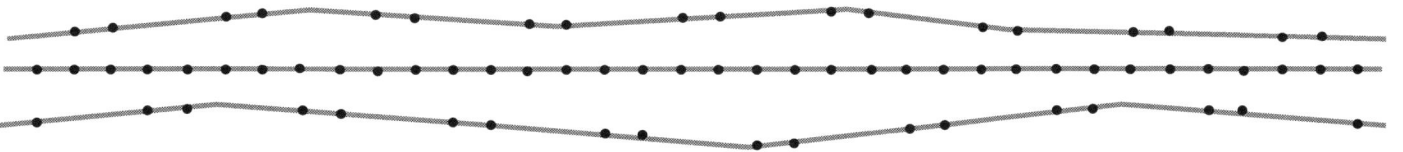

Number the clouds by size,
from smallest to largest.

1

2

3

4

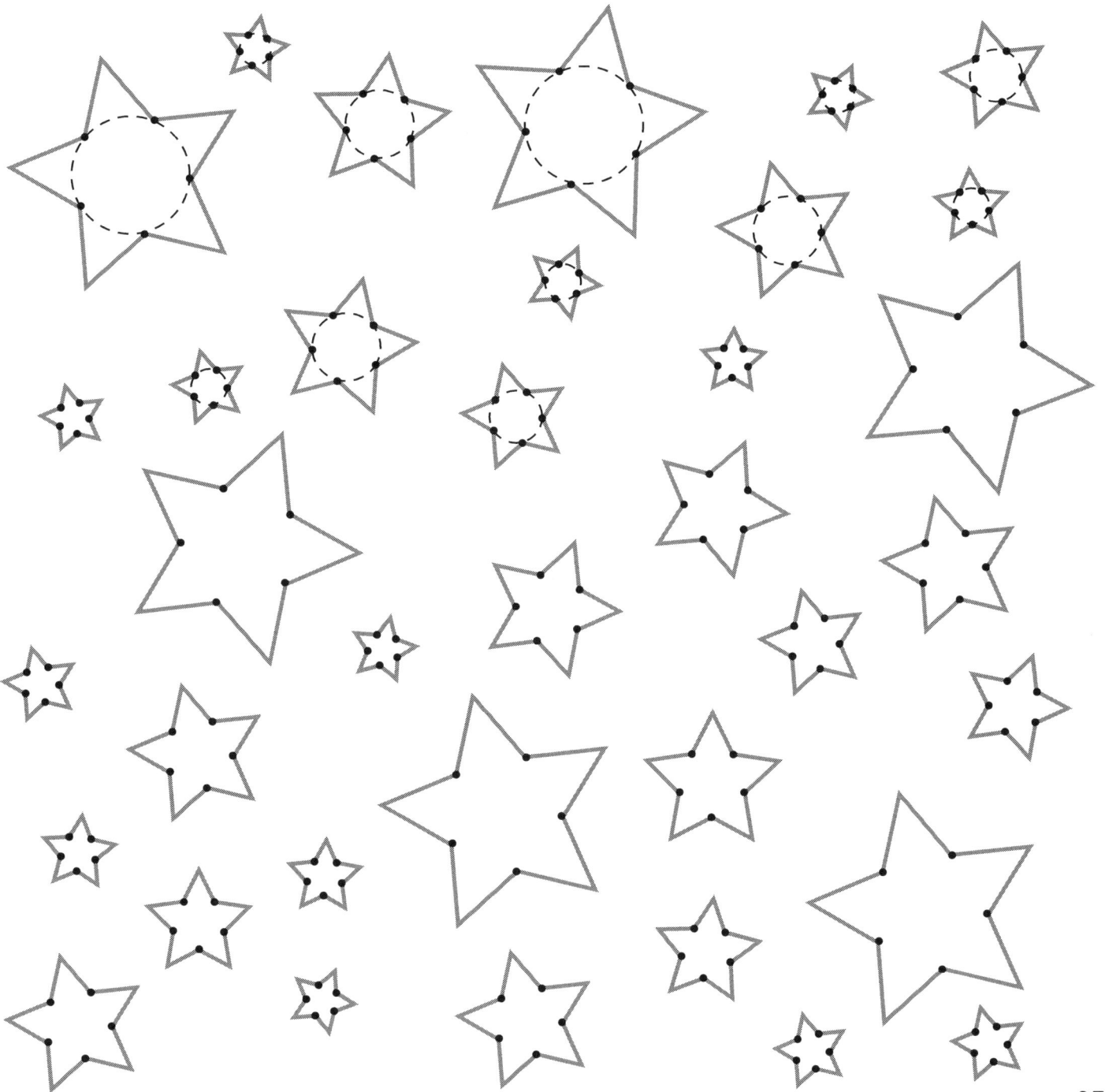

Match the halves of the ships correctly.

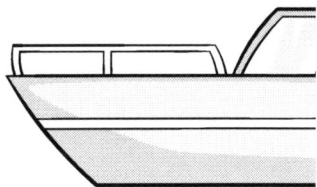

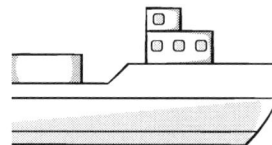

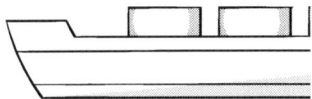

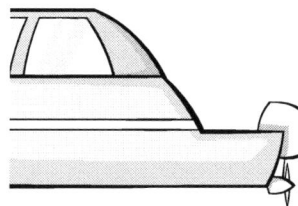

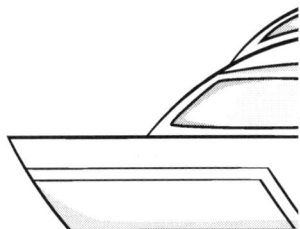

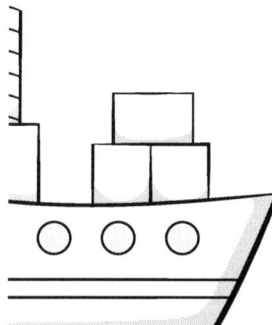

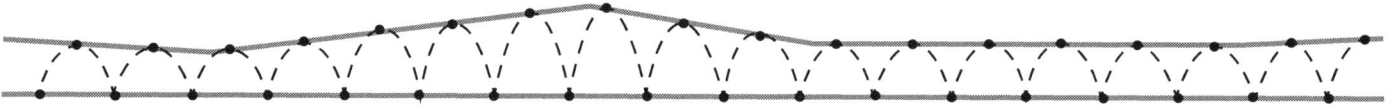

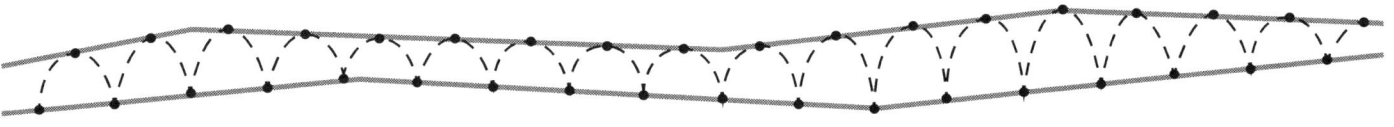

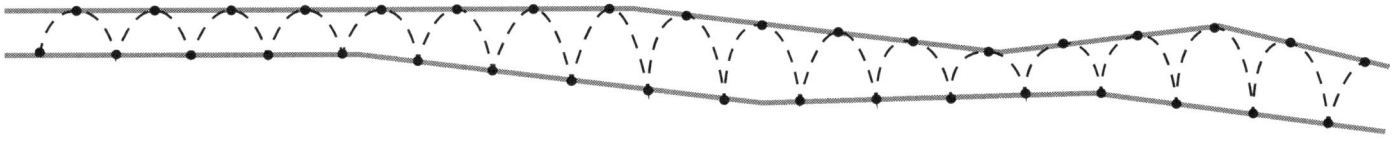

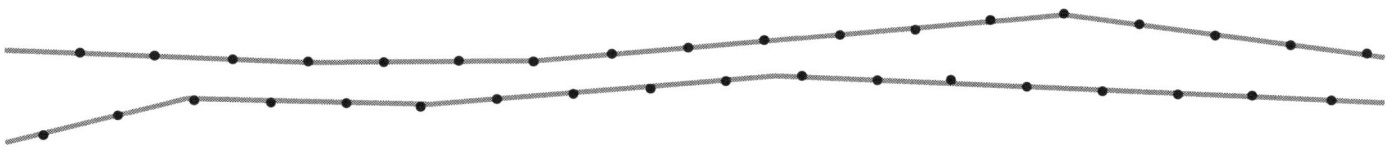

27

The boat
is sailing on the lake

Mark the fish of the same shape
with their corresponding numbers

1 2 3 4 5

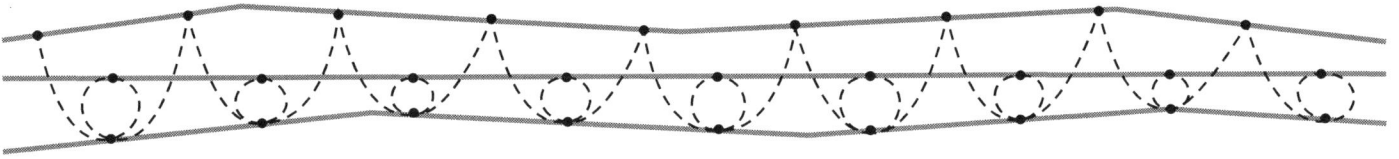

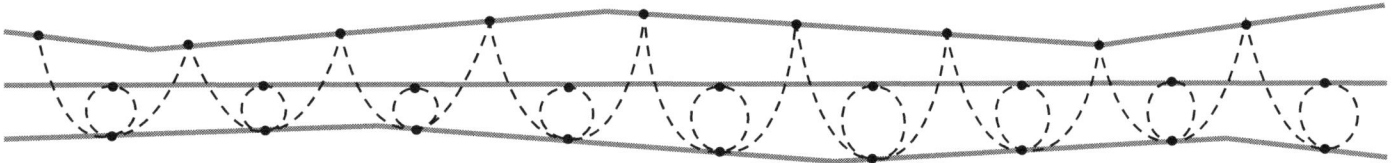

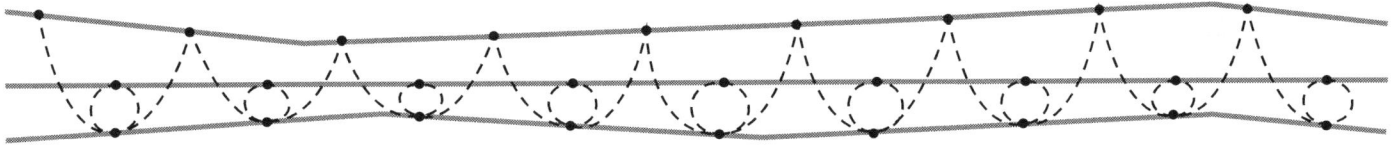

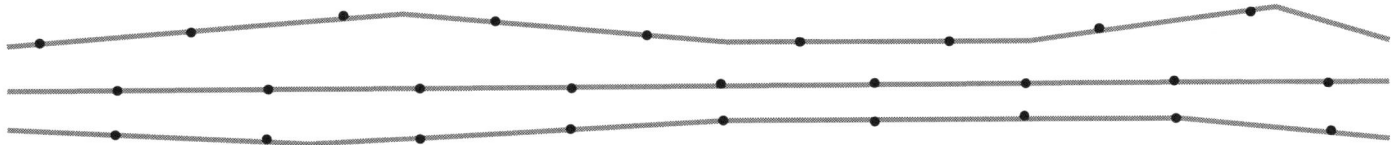

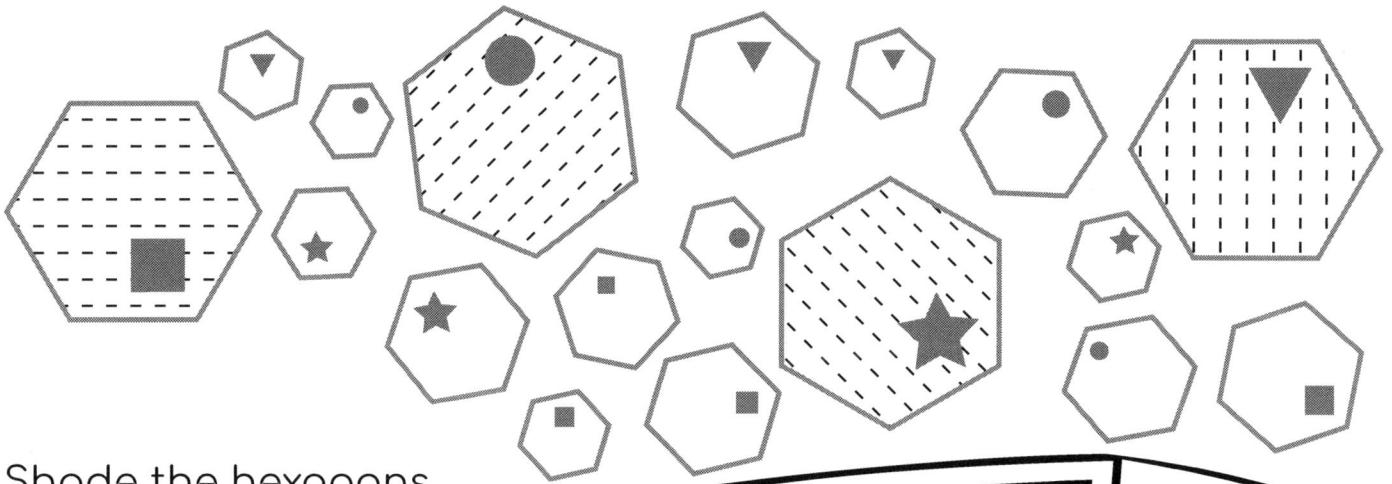

Shade the hexagons
according to the
sample.

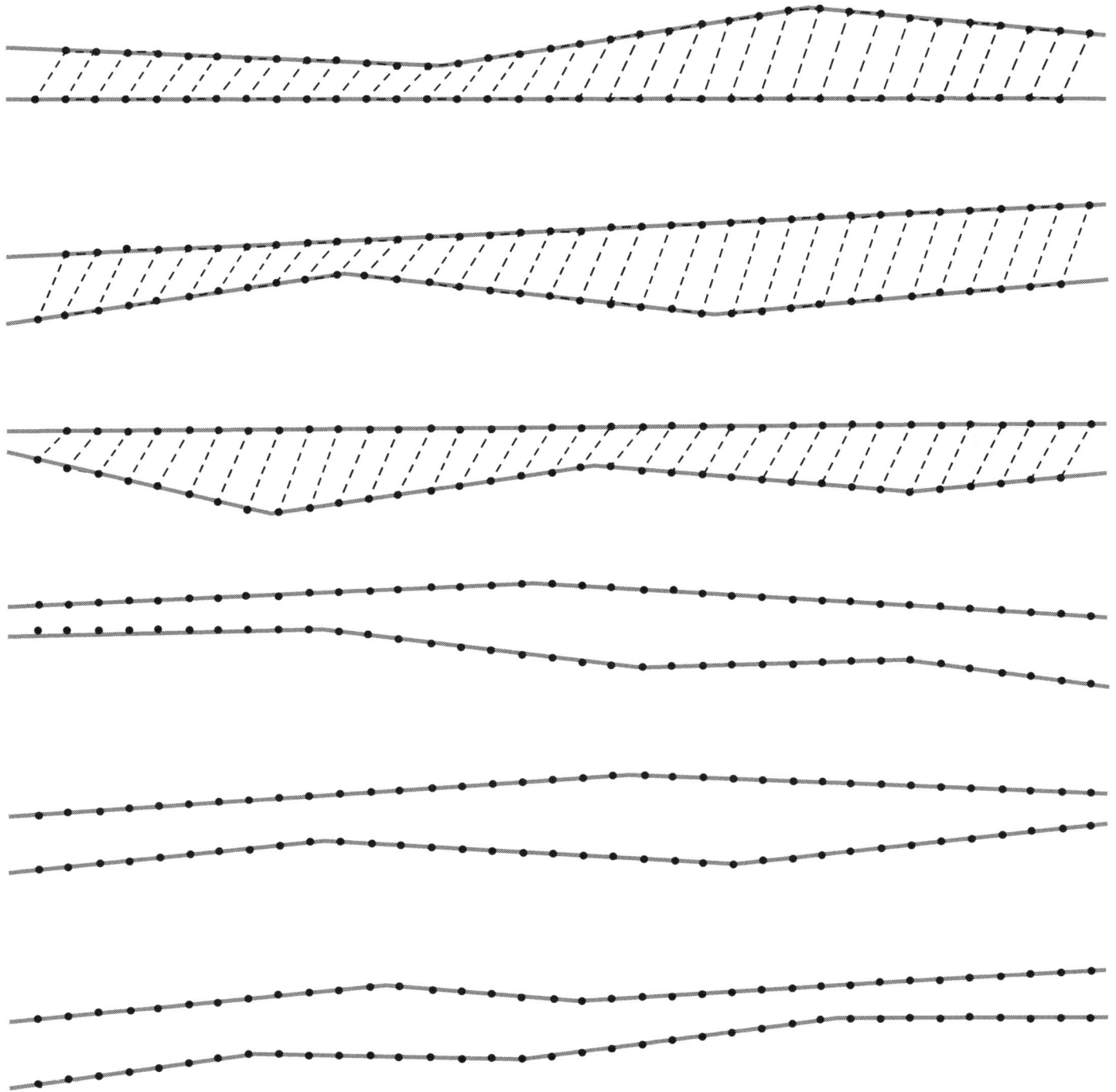

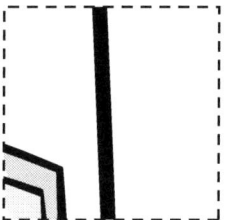

Repair the truck.

Cut out the squares and stick them in the correct places.

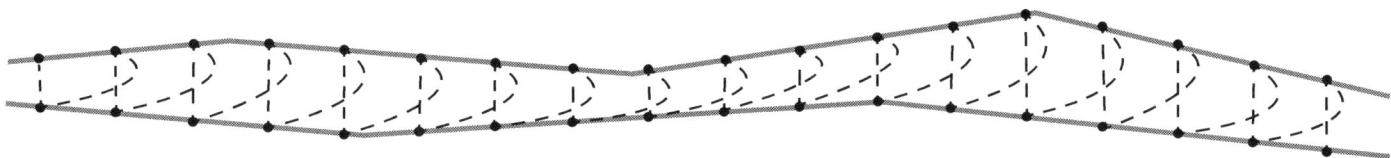

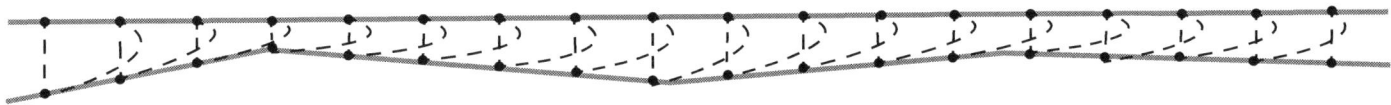

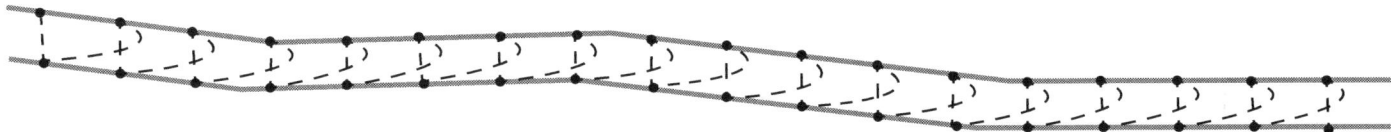

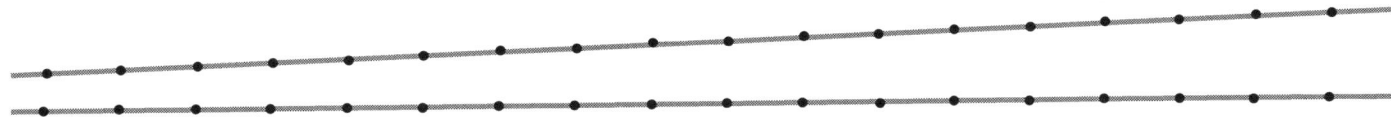

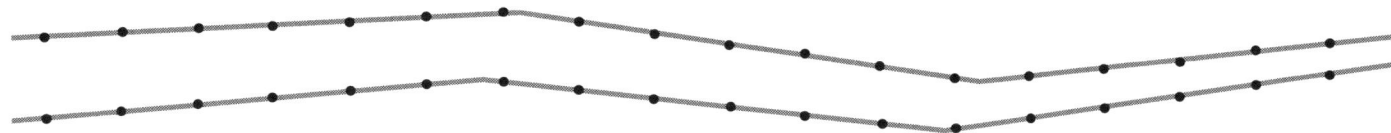

33

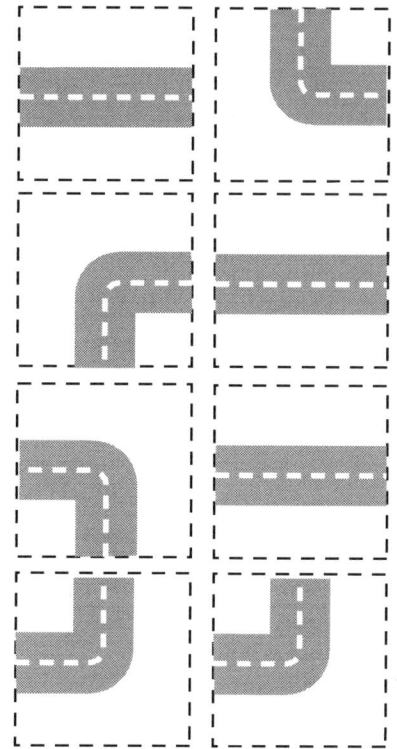

Help the scooter get home.

Cut out the parts of the road and glue them in the correct order.

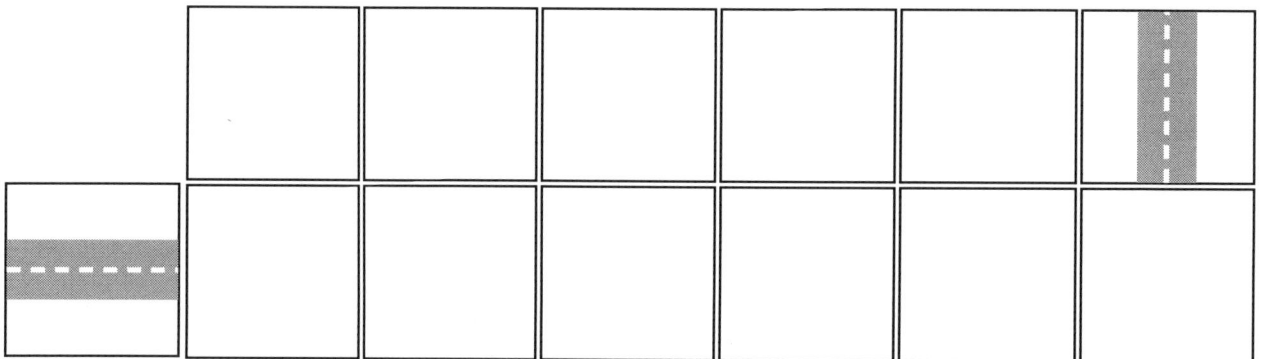

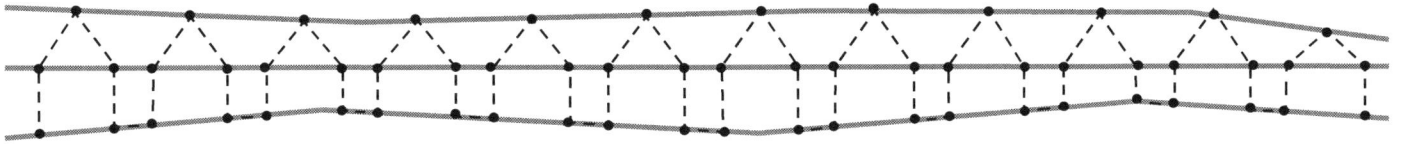

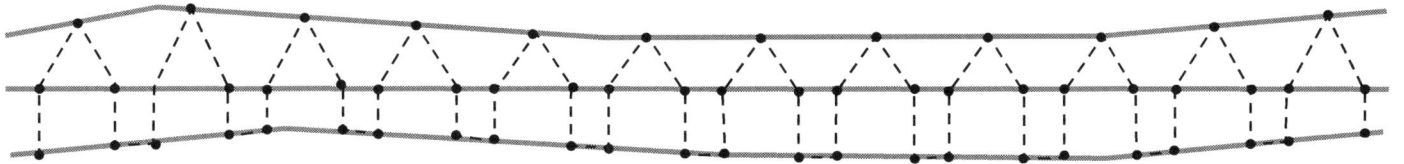

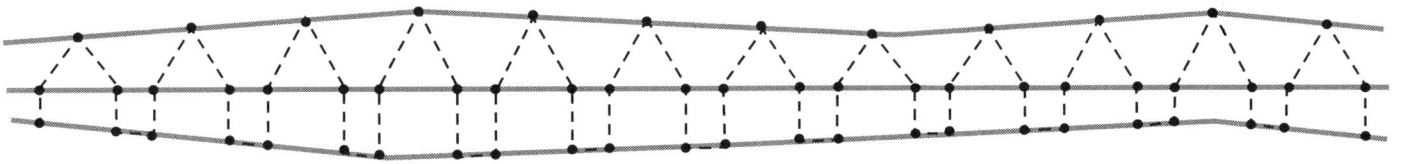

Match the halves of the transport correctly.

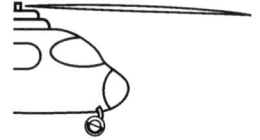

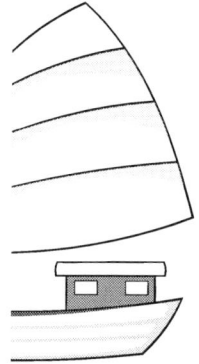

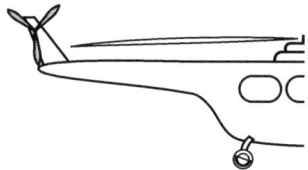

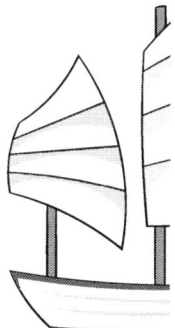

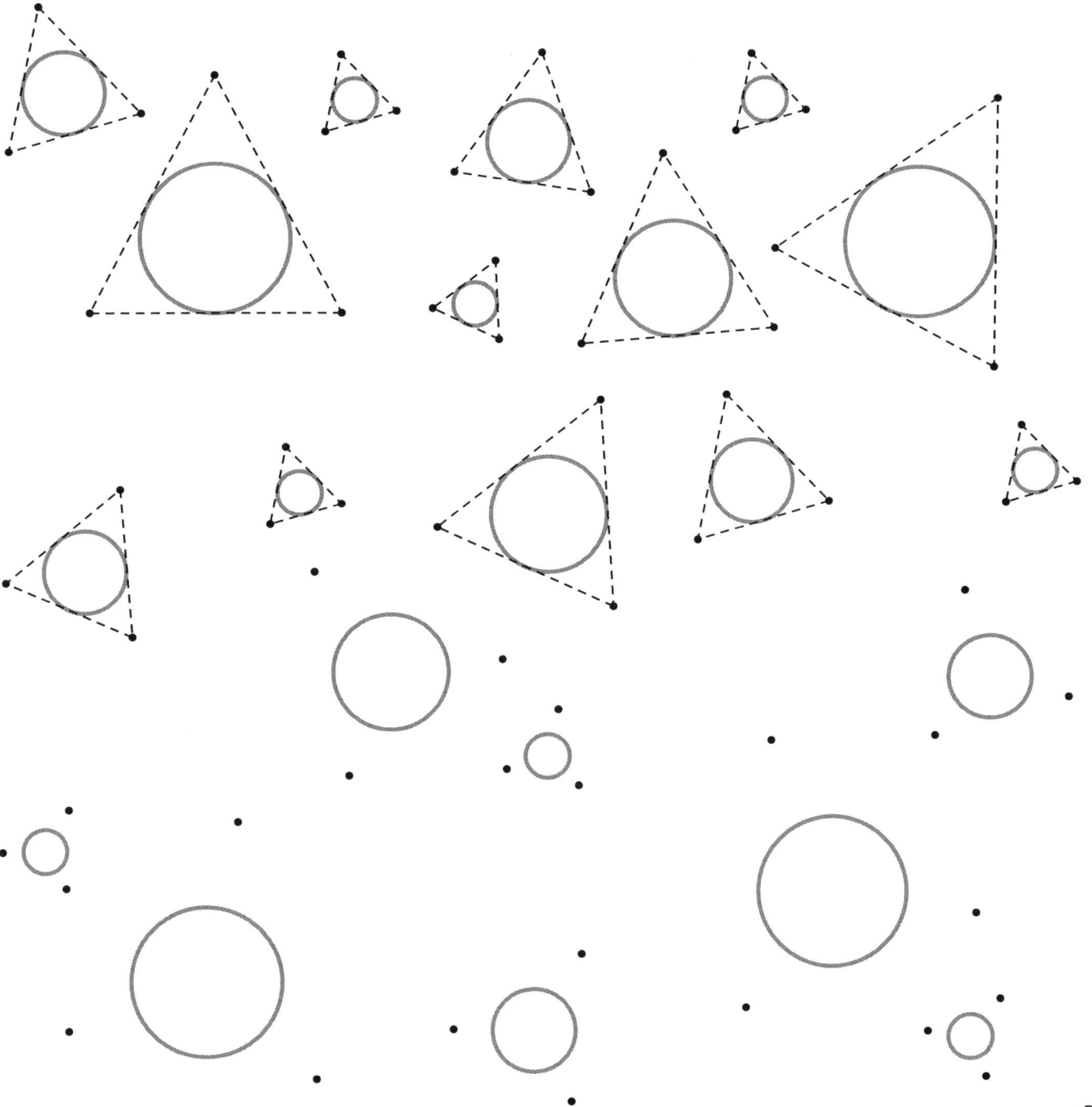

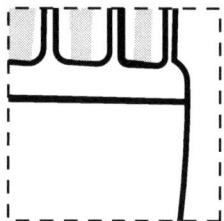

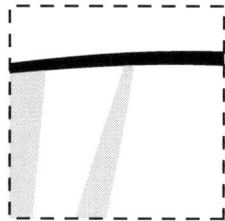

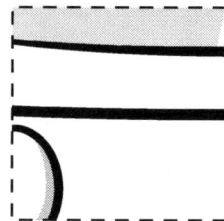

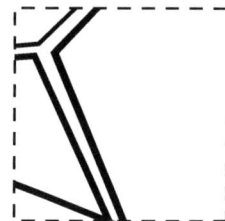

Repair the tram.

Cut out the squares and
stick them in the correct places.

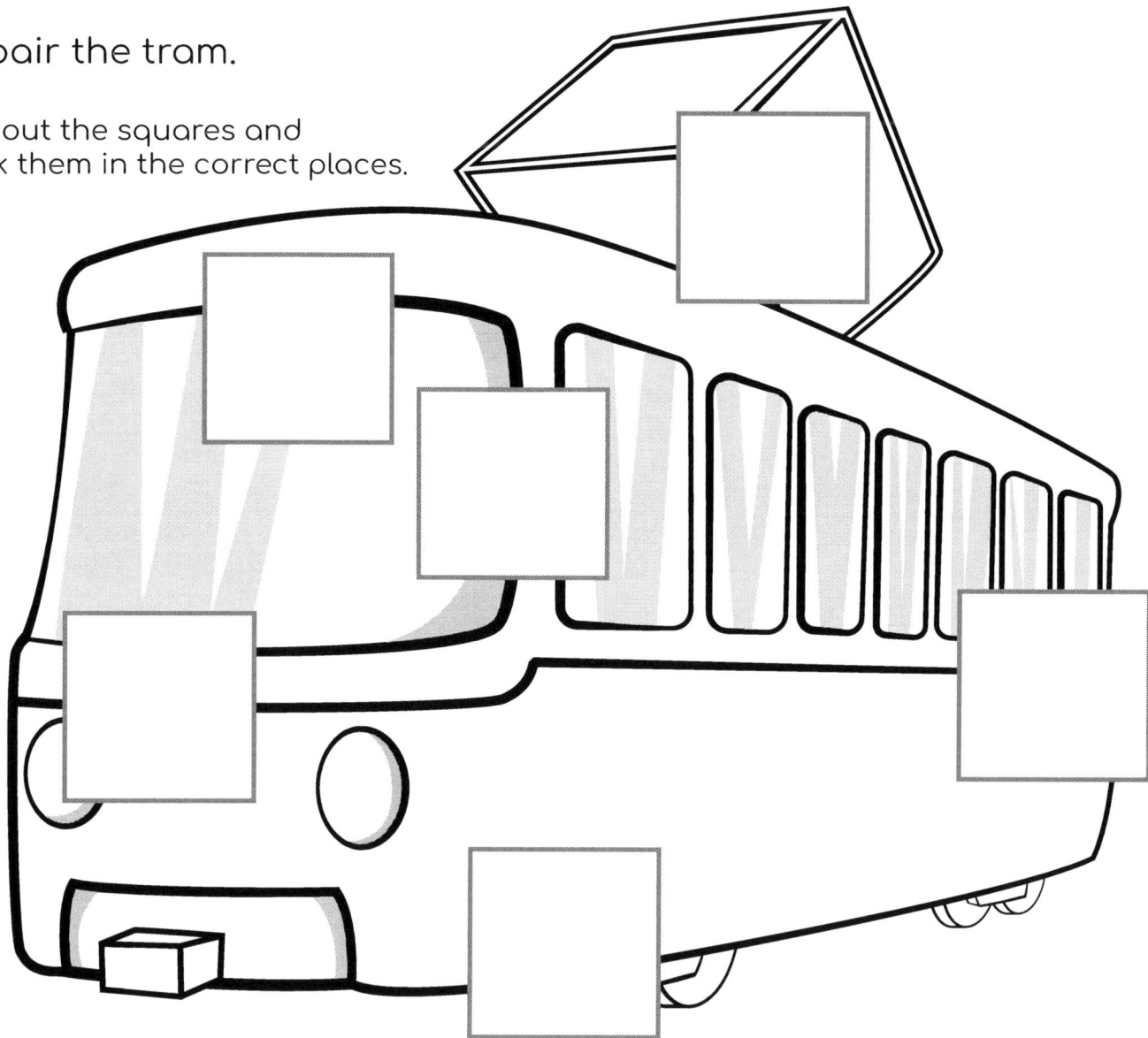

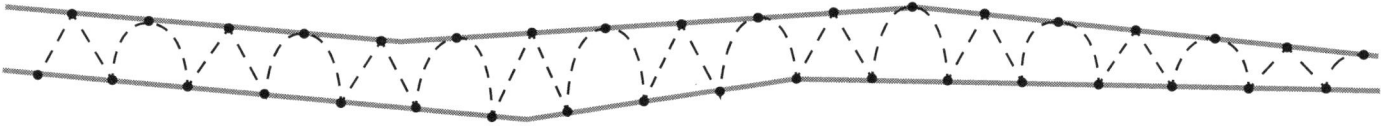

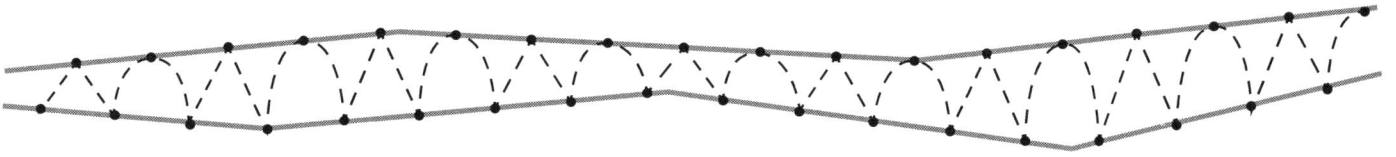

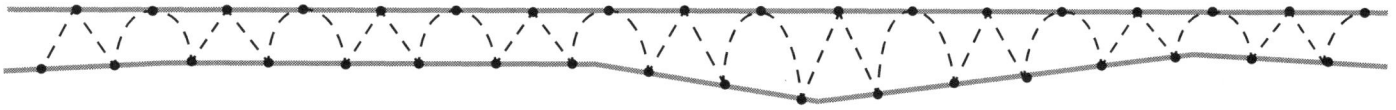

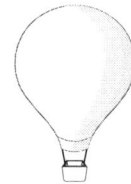

Find and color
the same balloons.

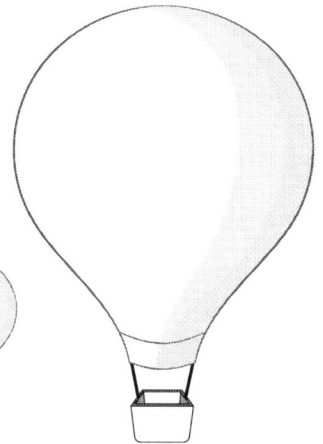

40

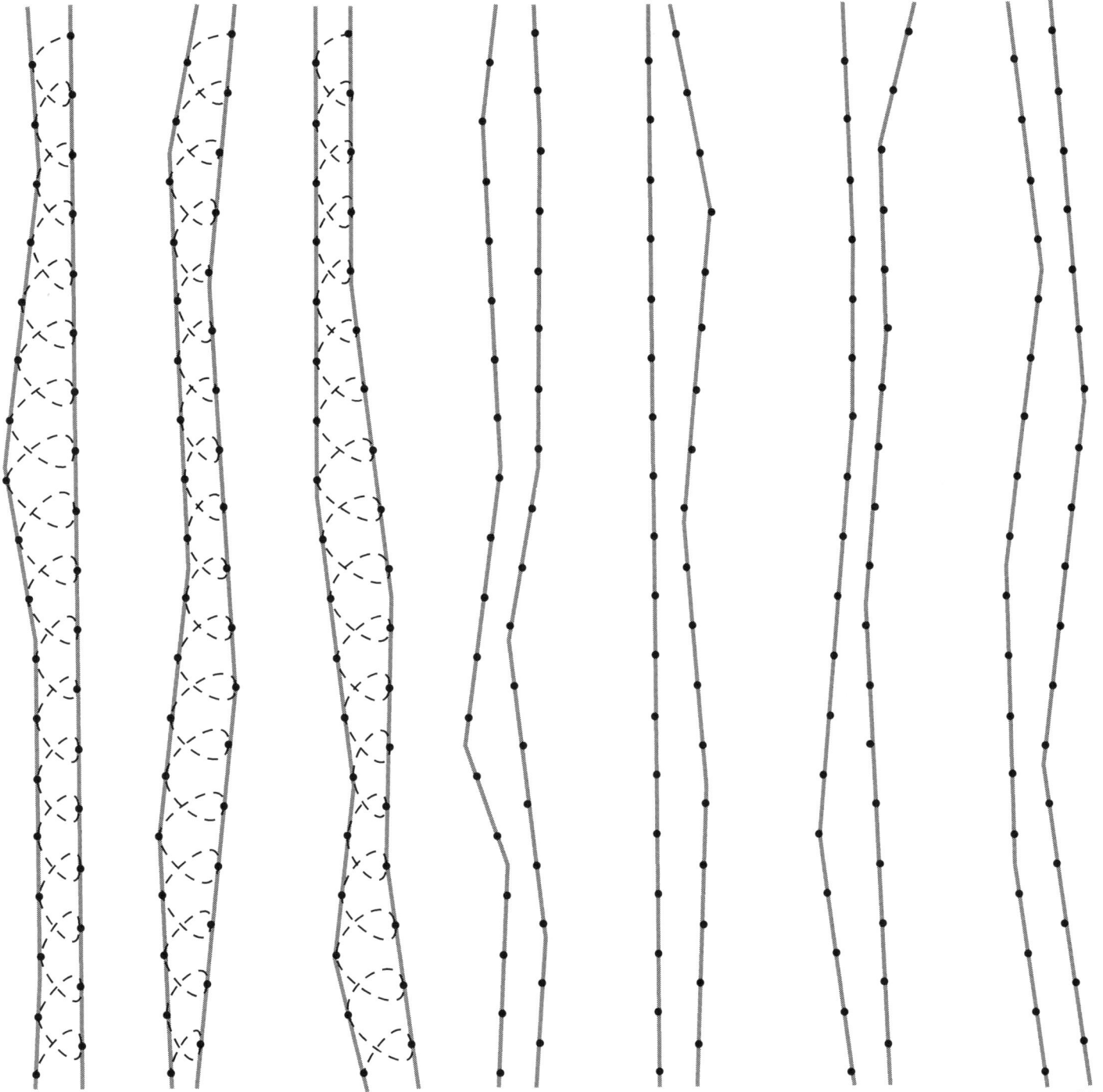

Made in the USA
Columbia, SC
13 July 2025